LIFE Books

EDITOR Robert Sullivan
DIRECTOR OF PHOTOGRAPHY Barbara Baker Burrows
CREATIVE DIRECTOR Richard Baker
DEPUTY PICTURE EDITOR Christina Lieberman
WRITER-REPORTER Hildegard Anderson
ART DIRECTOR Anke Stohlmann
COPY Danielle Dowling (Chief), Barbara Gogan
CONSULTING PICTURE EDITORS
Mimi Murphy (Rome), Tala Skari (Paris)

PRESIDENT Andrew Blau
BUSINESS MANAGER Roger Adler
BUSINESS DEVELOPMENT MANAGER Jeff Burak

EDITORIAL OPERATIONS Richard K. Prue,
David Sloan (Directors), Richard Shaffer (Group Manager),
Brian Fellows, Raphael Joa, Angel Mass,
Stanley E. Moyse, Albert Rufino (Managers), Soheila Asayesh, Keith Aurelio, Trang Ba Chuong,
Charlotte Coco, Osmar Escalona, Kevin Hart, Norma Jones, Mert Kerimoglu, Rosalie Khan, Marco Lau,
Po Fung Ng, Rudi Papiri, Barry Pribula,
Carina A. Rosario, Albert Rufino, Christopher Scala,
Diana Suryakusuma, Vaune Trachtman, Paul Tupay, Lionel Vargas, David Weiner

Time Inc. Home Entertainment

PUBLISHER Richard Fraiman
GENERAL MANAGER Steven Sandonato
EXECUTIVE DIRECTOR, MARKETING SERVICES
Carol Pittard
DIRECTOR, RETAIL & SPECIAL SALES Tom Mifsud
DIRECTOR, NEW PRODUCT DEVELOPMENT
Peter Harper
ASSISTANT DIRECTOR, BRAND MARKETING
Laura Adam
ASSOCIATE GENERAL COUNSEL
Helen Wan
BOOK PRODUCTION MANAGER Jonathan Polsky
DESIGN & PREPRESS MANAGER
Anne-Michelle Gallero
SENIOR BRAND MANAGER Joy Butts
ASSOCIATE BRAND MANAGER Shelley Rescober

Special thanks to Bozena Bannett,
Glenn Buonocore, Suzanne Janso, Robert Marasco, Brooke Reger, Mary Sarro-Waite,
Ilene Schreder, Adriana Tierno, Alex Voznesenskiy

Copyright 2008
Time Inc. HOME ENTERTAINMENT

LIFE Books

Time Inc., 1271 Avenue of the Americas,
New York, NY 10020

ISBN 10: 1-60320-011-8
ISBN 13: 978-1-60320-011-0
Library of Congress Control Number: 2007910090

Printed in China

"**LIFE**" is a trademark of Time Inc.

We welcome your comments and suggestions about LIFE Books.
Please write to us at:
LIFE Books
Attention: Book Editors
PO Box 11016
Des Moines, IA 50336-1016
If you would like to order any of our hardcover Collector's Edition books, please call us at 1-800-327-6388 (Monday
through Friday, 7:00 a.m.–8:00 p.m., or Saturday, 7:00 a.m.–6:00 p.m., Central Time).

NATURE'S FURY

CONTENTS

Front cover: On September 8, 1999, lightning fills the sky above San Francisco.
Douglas Keister/Corbis

Back cover: A section of New Orleans just east of downtown is submerged in the wake of Hurricane Katrina on August 30, 2005.
Smiley N. Pool/Dallas Morning News

Endpapers: At Hawaii Volcanoes National Park in 1997, the lava flow from Kilauea's Puu Oo vent creates a surreal mosaic. Kilauea is perhaps the most active volcano in the world.
G. Brad Lewis/Getty

Title page: In the aftermath of the 1906 earthquake that rocked San Francisco, a brand-new crevasse in Marin County, just across the Golden Gate Bridge, is a point of interest.
Courtesy of the Bancroft Library

Previous spread: A supercell thunderstorm, producing lightning and baseball-size hail, dominates the sky over the Kansas plains in the summer of 2005.
Jim Reed/Photo Resources

Right: On May 18, 1980, an onrushing ash cloud from the eruption of Washington State's Mount St. Helens spurs a frantic flight.
Kevin Millican

Introduction

IN ANCIENT TIMES
Imagining the Violent World of Yesteryear

The earth emerged from cataclysm 4.5 billion years ago and has been evolving ever since. Natural forces beneath its crust and millions of miles beyond its atmosphere are forever affecting life on our planet. Eruptions are constant, as are changes in climate. Our daily weather is ruled by the sun: Every sublime summer morning and every brutal winter blizzard are products of the sun's energy impacting our atmosphere from 93 million miles away. The weather shapes the earth's landscape, in turn, but it's not the only element working on the topography. As the planet's tectonic plates shift—as fissures are created that tap into our molten core 1,800 miles down—the thermal power of the earth's underworld is unleashed. The planet quakes. Mountains explode into the sky. It has always been thus.

Yes, there is vigorous debate about mankind's influence—or lack thereof—on global warming and climate change. But whether violent weather has become more intense or frequent is not the point we are addressing here. What we are concerned with is not the effect man may be having on the planet but the historical record of what Mother Nature has meted out to it. Nature has raged all about this little sphere of ours for, as Carl Sagan would have said, billions and billions of years. Earth has been buffeted and flooded, frozen and thawed. And at the end of the long, long day, nature has delivered us these gifts: our precious planet and life itself. Even as we bewail tragedies that occasionally afflict us—the killer storms, the fiery lava flows—we should remember that the forces behind these catastrophes are also responsible for why we are here in the first place. We can call it nature's fury, but it is really just nature's way.

HAVING A BIG IMPACT Collisions with asteroids and comets not unlike Comet West changed our planet aeons ago.

In the beginning, there was a flaming mass, then the cooling, then the comet assaults that formed the oceans, then life and five mass extinctions, and, of course, the formings and separations and reformings of a super-continent, plus the subtle changes in the earth's orbit that triggered the occasional ice age....

The disappearance of the dinosaurs is a good place to start when considering the enormous sway nature holds over progress on our planet, because it allows us to visualize the chaos. For 160 million years they thrived, first on the single landmass Pangaea and then, as it split apart, on several smaller continents. The fossil record tells us the great creatures died out quite suddenly 65 million years ago, but it doesn't tell us precisely why. Some scientists think a climactic shift at the end of the Mesozoic

THE NATURAL ORDER Dinosaurs (**above**) were the kings of the food chain until, for whatever reason, they weren't. **Opposite:** God told Noah that a flood was coming and asked him to save the animals.

Era doomed the beasts, but others say this transformation occurred so slowly that the animals would have simply migrated to more suitable situations. Did a faster-moving catastrophe bring about their demise? Perhaps volcanic hyperactivity created a global cloud of lethal carbon dioxide. Maybe the dust from a gigantic asteroid strike blackened the skies and caused temperatures to plummet. Whatever the reason, nature was sensationally furious.

The many subsequent natural calamities that fill our planet's history did not lack for the spectacular either. Imagine, if you will, the most recent ice age, which surged toward the Mason-Dixon Line 18,000 years ago. The summit of New Hampshire's Mount Washington, which today stands more than a mile above sea level, was buried under ice. Most of Pennsylvania, Ohio and Illinois was blanketed by a large white sheet.

Imagine Noah's flood: "And the rain was upon the earth 40 days and 40 nights," the Book of Genesis tells us. The flooding lasted even longer, and Noah's ark was borne upon the waves. Finally, "God made a wind to pass over the earth, and the waters assuaged," causing the ark to settle "upon the mountains of Ararat." Scores of archaeological searches for evidence of this flood—*the* flood—have proved inconclusive. Some teams have sought for proof of a universal deluge of truly earth-shattering proportions in the centuries before Christ's birth, while others have looked for signs of a large local flood in the area near Mount Ararat in Turkey—to no certain avail. However, that no one has yet substantiated the Bible's account does not alter the fact that the writers

EINZUG IN DIE ARCHE.   ENTRY IN THE ARK.

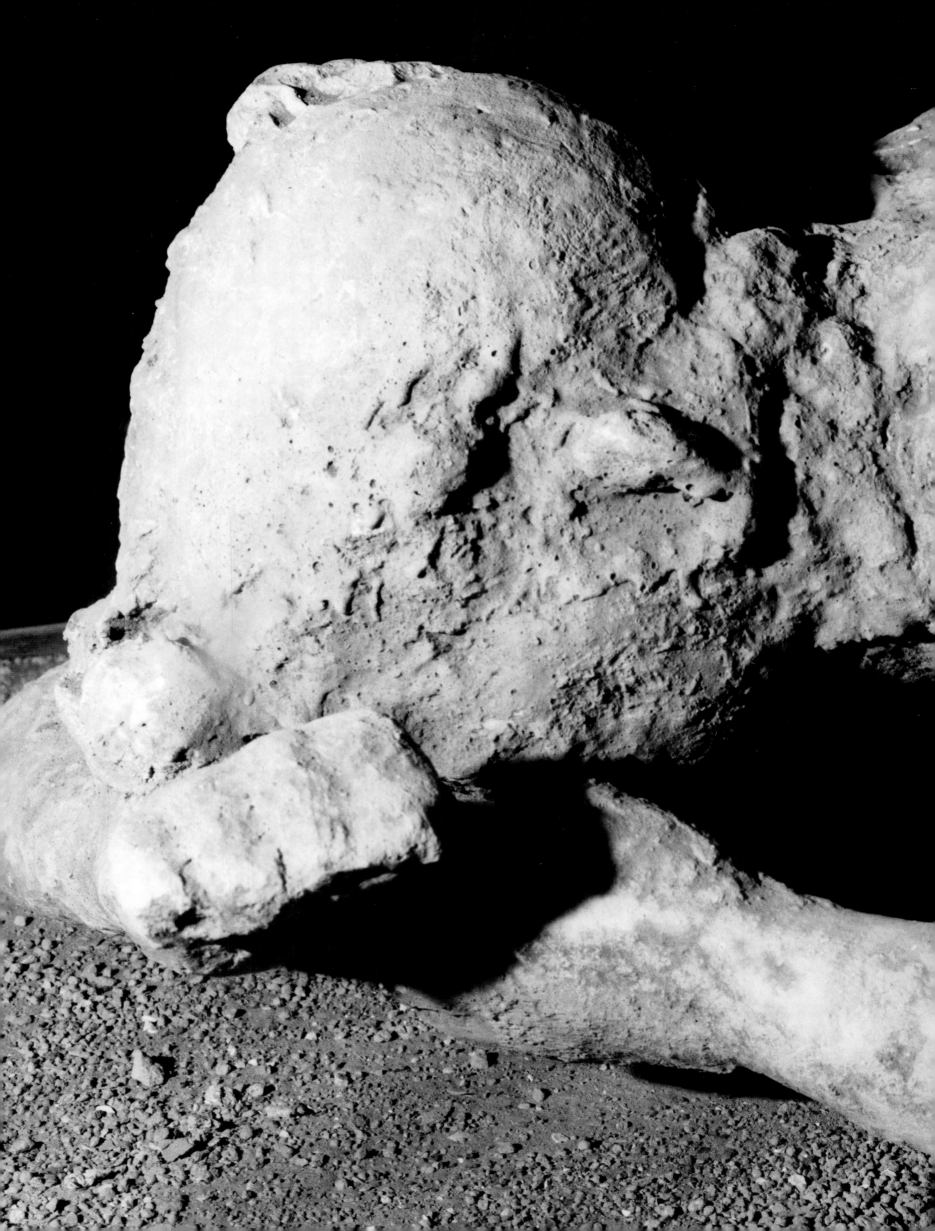

of Scripture knew what a torrential flood looked like and the power it possessed to destroy all in its path.

Imagine, next, the great—and terrible—volcanic explosions of ages past. Four historic blasts stand out, and for our purposes, it is useful to compare what occurred on the Mediterranean island of Thera (now called Santorini), on Italy's Mount Vesuvius and on the two Indonesian islands of Sumbawa and Krakatau.

We can only guess what happened on Thera since nothing about the event, which took place circa 1470 B.C., exists in the written historical record. After examining the evidence, archaeologists are certain that the ring of five islands now known as Santorini were once part of a single island that was 10 miles wide and dominated by a mountain nearly a mile high. The top of that mountain exploded in titanic fashion nearly 3,500 years ago, covering the island in ash and sending a tsunami as high as 300 feet crashing against the cliffs of Crete some 70 miles to the south. The sonic boom that was emitted could be heard deep in the African jungle and along the Scandinavian shore. Thirty-two cubic miles of Thera were ultimately obliterated, and damage elsewhere throughout the Mediterranean was surely tremendous. Some have speculated that the enormity of the calamity might have contributed to the swift decline of Crete's sophisticated Minoan civilization. Others have theorized that stories of what occurred on Thera, handed down by word of mouth, were the model for Plato's history of the lost wonderland called Atlantis.

The eruption of the 6,000-foot Mount Vesuvius near the Bay of Naples at one p.m. on August 24 in A.D. 79 wreaked havoc on a second refined culture, that of the Romans who lived in the splendid seaside

THE MOMENT ITSELF A Pompeiian victim of Vesuvius's wrath testifies, all these centuries later, as to how fast nature can strike.

cities of Herculaneum and Pompeii. Right up until it blew, Vesuvius, dormant for 1,500 years, looked like the epitome of a scenic, graceful peak, with the olive groves on its lower slopes accenting its considerable sublimity. Then suddenly, Vesuvius became a literal hell on earth. From its angry cone, fiery ash and pumice were propelled 12 miles into the sky. Terror and death fell upon wealthy vacationers in the resorts of Herculaneum and on farmers in the fields outside Pompeii. As many as 30,000 people were either buried alive under as much as 50 feet of ash or were asphyxiated by carbon monoxide. Today, the plaster casts of these Roman citizens in their death throes are perhaps the world's most poignant memorials to victims of natural disasters.

As had been the case with Vesuvius, the verdant Mount Tambora on the Indonesian island of Sumbawa

THE PAST MADE CLEAR Within the curvature of this Santorini isle, the formerly immense single island can be envisioned.

was presumed extinct, until, in early April 1815, the 13,000-foot mountain began to shake. In the planet's largest eruption since the end of the last ice age, the island exploded with a force of between 20,000 and 25,000 megatons. Nine hundred miles away, a sea captain thought he heard cannon fire and readied his ship, believing he would soon be mixing it up with pirates. The top half of Tambora—more than a mile of mountain—blew literally sky-high. Some 170 billion tons of volcanic debris shot into the atmosphere, and as far as 300 miles away, darkness reigned for three days. Ten thousand Sumbawans were killed instantly; 80,000 more Indonesians died because of the resultant famine and disease. The ash cloud roamed, affecting everything. "The year without a summer" followed in 1816. It snowed in Vermont in July. A killing frost ruined farms in Connecticut in August.

Firsthand accounts of Tambora's eruption are rare. Less rare are reports of a second 19th-century cataclysm in Indonesia. When the triple-cone volcanic island Krakatau, lying between Java and Sumatra, exploded in 1883, many witnessed the horror, which had been foreshadowed by weeks of dark smoke billowing from the highest, 6,000-foot summit. The eloquent classicist J.V. Luce wrote in his book *Lost Atlantis* of the climactic moment of Monday, August 27, at 10:02 a.m.: "The sound of the explosion was heard over an enormous area. Blast waves broke windows and cracked walls up to 160 kilometers off." The explosion was heard 3,000 miles away in Madagascar; it was judged to be the loudest sound in recorded history. "Krakatoa [Luce used the old spelling] has no rival in the extreme violence of its culminating paroxysms, and in the catastrophic air- and sea-waves to which it gave rise." Nine hours after the eruption, a tsunami traveling at 400 miles per hour slammed into the harbor at Calcutta. Luce wrote: "The tidal waves were extremely destructive. Nearly 300 towns and villages bordering the Sunda Strait were devastated, and 36,380 people lost their lives.... Owing to the darkness and terror, reliable observation of the height of the waves was almost impossible. They are thought to have reached 36 meters in places.... The after-effects of the great 1883 eruption finally faded away in sunsets and after-glows of striking beauty which were noted all over Europe and America during the winter months."

We imagine comets rushing toward the earth...imagine the death of the dinosaurs...imagine the many ice ages...the floods...imagine the eruptions and the tsunamis...imagine the storms.

Shakespeare himself imagined them—or at least one particular storm—and thereby immortalized, in his final play, *The Tempest,* the first hurricane of significance in American history. This story has everything: wind, waves, lots of Sturm und Drang, even celebrities.

By the early 17th century (the summer of 1609, to be specific), Britain had begun its colonization of North America, Shakespeare was the darling of London's cultural elite, and an outsize gale was blowing in the mid-Atlantic. Setting sail from England to the nascent and faltering British settlement at Jamestown was a fleet of nine ships with more than 500 potential colonists and provisions vital to the outpost. The hurricane surged into the fleet and scattered the ships. One vessel went down, while seven others struggled on to America. Historians have written that this mission was, in hindsight, crucial to the colony's survival, so we are left to wonder: If the entire fleet had been wiped out, would Jamestown have perished then and there? Would England have given up its colonial designs on the New World just as they were getting under way? If nature had done a more thorough job, would we be we?

But what of the ninth vessel? The flagship, *Sea Venture,* was tossed for three days by the storm. The hull was gashed; crewmen stuffed leaks with anything available, even meat from the larder. The sailors bailed water and threw luggage overboard in an effort to remain, if barely, afloat. Some of the terrified folks were making peace with their God when the ship ran aground off the uninhabited archipelago we now call Bermuda. One hundred fifty souls boarded lifeboats and made for shore.

We know the details of this storm because of a vivid account written by William Strachey, the expedition's secretary. "And the ship in every joint almost, having spewed out her oakum, before we were aware was grown five foot suddenly deep with water," Strachey wrote at one point. "[A]nd we almost drowned within, whiles we sat looking when to perish from above. This imparting no less terror than danger, ran through the whole ship...."

Strachey was among those who, within a year, ventured on to Jamestown in one of two boats that the survivors

built on Bermuda. A second passenger who pressed on to North America was none other than John Rolfe, who, through his romance with the Powhatan princess Pocahontas, became a seminal figure in European-American relations and an early hero in the great American saga.

Yet another noted personality involved in this tale was the Earl of Southampton, Shakespeare's patron and Strachey's friend. Did the earl share Strachey's story with the bard? Did Strachey, as some accounts have it, know Shakespeare personally? Well, consider that Strachey wrote of many bats on Bermuda, and the characters in *The Temptest* "go a-bat fowling." Strachey reported that during the storm the *Sea Venture*'s captain saw Saint Elmo's fire, a sailor's good-luck charm: "An apparition of a little round light, like a faint star, trembling and streaming along with a sparkling blaze, half the height upon the main mast, and shooting sometimes from shroud to shroud . . . half the night, it kept with us, running sometimes along the main yard to the very end and then returning." Two years later, in 1611, when *The Tempest* was first staged in London, Shakespeare's sprite Ariel said:

"Now on the beak,

Now in the waist, the deck, in every cabin,

I flamed amazement: sometime I'd divide,

And burn in many places; on the topmast,

The yards and bowsprit; would I flame distinctly,

Then meet and join."

We're discussing this hurricane story at length not only because it features such historical luminaries as Shakespeare, John Rolfe and Pocahontas, but also because we are, in this introduction to *Nature's Fury,* engaged in the act of imagining, and the accounts of bygone writers help us acutely picture what might have happened in the Atlantic in 1609. Shortly, we will see nature's fury firsthand, through 25 dramatic events that have occurred since the advent of photography. Cameras record many things well, but

GRANGER

they record few things as dramatically as they do natural calamity. What you will see on the pages that follow really happened, in our time or the time of our immediate forebears. You won't believe your eyes.

But you must—and as you do, you should remember (and this is the principal point of our preface): The events you gaze upon are only the tip of the iceberg, merely the latest news. So much else has happened, long-ago events with no Shakespeare to do them justice.

There was another hurricane, in 1780, that roared through the Caribbean, demolishing both the British and French fleets, which, at the time, were involved in the American Revolution, and claiming 22,000 lives—the deadliest storm in our country's history.

There have been other volcanic eruptions. Several examples can be taken from a single entity, one so reliable it will probably provide fur-

GEORGE RODGER

ther evidence any day now. Rising 10,000 feet above the sea on the Italian island of Sicily, Mount Etna vents between 10 and 20 times per century, with lava flowing down its slopes and a white plume of smoke rising from its summit. It has fully erupted more than 200 times in all. The explosion of 1169 was bad, that of 1669 even worse. Several villages were buried under lava, and the island's second-largest city, Catania, was decimated. A low estimate is that 20,000 people were killed, but the number is probably much closer to 100,000. Vesuvius, which is not very far away, remains regularly active as well.

There have been earthquakes, the deadliest of them taking many more lives than do volcanoes. There are half a million detectable earthquakes recorded in the world annually—10,000 in Southern California alone. The rumblings of 100,000 of these can be felt by man, and perhaps 100 cause damage. So clearly, most earthquakes have been forgotten, but the giants have left an awful mark. In 1556, an earthquake in China's Shaanxi province killed 830,000 people, the greatest of four earthquakes in China that have claimed more than 200,000 lives. The so-called Killer Quake in Antioch in A.D. 526 wiped out as many as 300,000 people. And many earthquakes have spawned tsunamis. Japan has been particularly plagued by the giant waves, having suffered 195 of them since the first one was recorded in the Kii Channel in A.D. 684. Quakes and tsunamis in 1854 killed up to 100,000 Japanese.

There have been, if we're seeking disasters even more lethal than earthquakes, floods—floods of, to hark back

YESTERDAY, AND TODAY The *Sea Venture* (**opposite**) wrecks in 1609. Vesuvius (**above**) stirs in 1944—and could tomorrow.

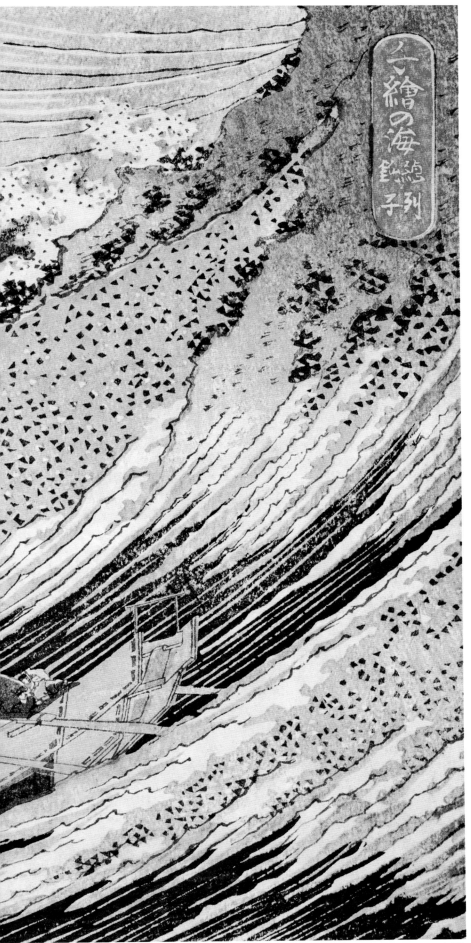

to Noah, biblical proportions. China has experienced no fewer than four floods that have led to death tolls of more than 300,000. As we will see later in the book, one of the three terrible floodings of the Huang He may have killed as many as 4 million people.

There have been avalanches, some generated by weather, some by the same forces that cause the earth to quake. In 218 B.C., Hannibal lost 18,000 of his soldiers, 2,000 horses and many elephants to avalanches in the Alps as he crossed those mighty mountains to engage the Roman Army. In 1618, the Rodi avalanche buried the village of Plurs, Switzerland, and its 1,500 inhabitants; the final death toll throughout the region was 2,427. In 1800, Napoleon Bonaparte, also marching toward Italy as Hannibal had many centuries earlier, lost 56 of his men in the French Alps when they were covered by 50 feet of snow.

There have been tornadoes. Whether we call them the Finger of God or the Tail of the Devil, they are horrific to behold on a horizon and often leave death in their wake, as they did in February 1884, when a series of them killed more than 600 people in the American South. On May 27, 1896, a tornado roared into the city of St. Louis and left 255 dead.

There have been, over these 4.5 billion action-packed years, events on a millennial, annual, monthly, weekly and daily basis. There have been things happening every minute.

Yes, there have been, in the past, multitudinous events—and we can only imagine them. There have been, in more recent times, other occurrences that can be recalled through pictures. Turn the page to see what it looks like…when nature turns furious.

PLAGUED Asia dominates deadly disaster lists—especially China with its earthquakes and floods and Japan with its tsunamis (**left**).

NATURE'S FURY
Cataclysms of the Modern Age

On April 18, 1935, a dust storm overwhelms
Stratford, Texas. In just a few more pages, you
will read more about the notorious Dust Bowl
that plagued the United States in the 1930s.

In the summer of 1972, a spectacular electrical storm is captured in a one-minute time-lapse photograph at the Kitt Peak National Observatory in Sells, Ariz.

On October 24, 2005, Hurricane Wilma sends titanic waves crashing over the seawall in Havana, flooding El Malecon Boulevard.

Seen from the village of Deles in central Java, Indonesia, on June 18, 2006, the summit of the Mount Merapi volcano blazes against the sky.

Green fields, a rainbow and an elegant fun-
nel make for a beautiful picture. But the fact
is that on June 12, 2004, in Mulvane, Kan.,
this F3 twister is poised to destroy a house.

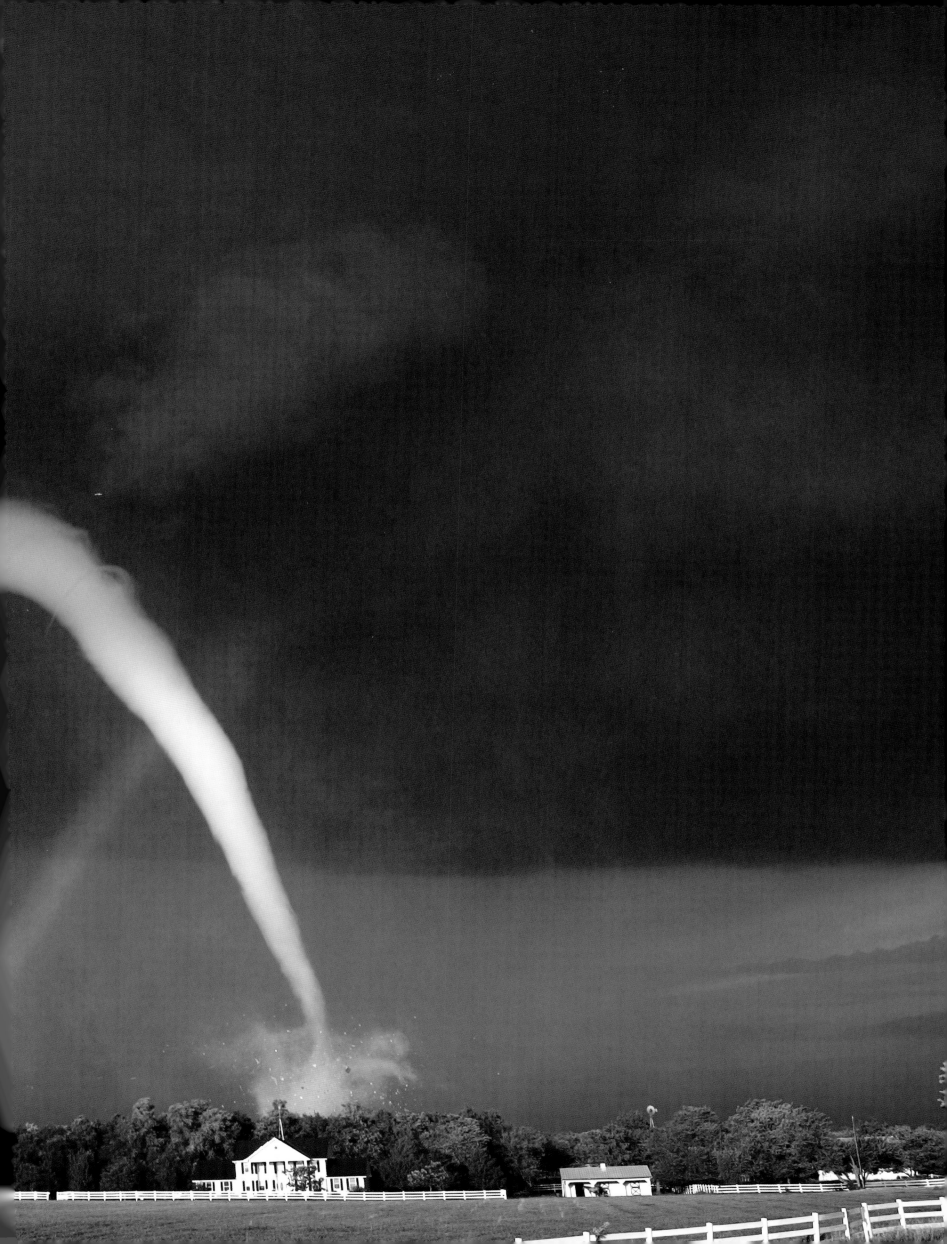

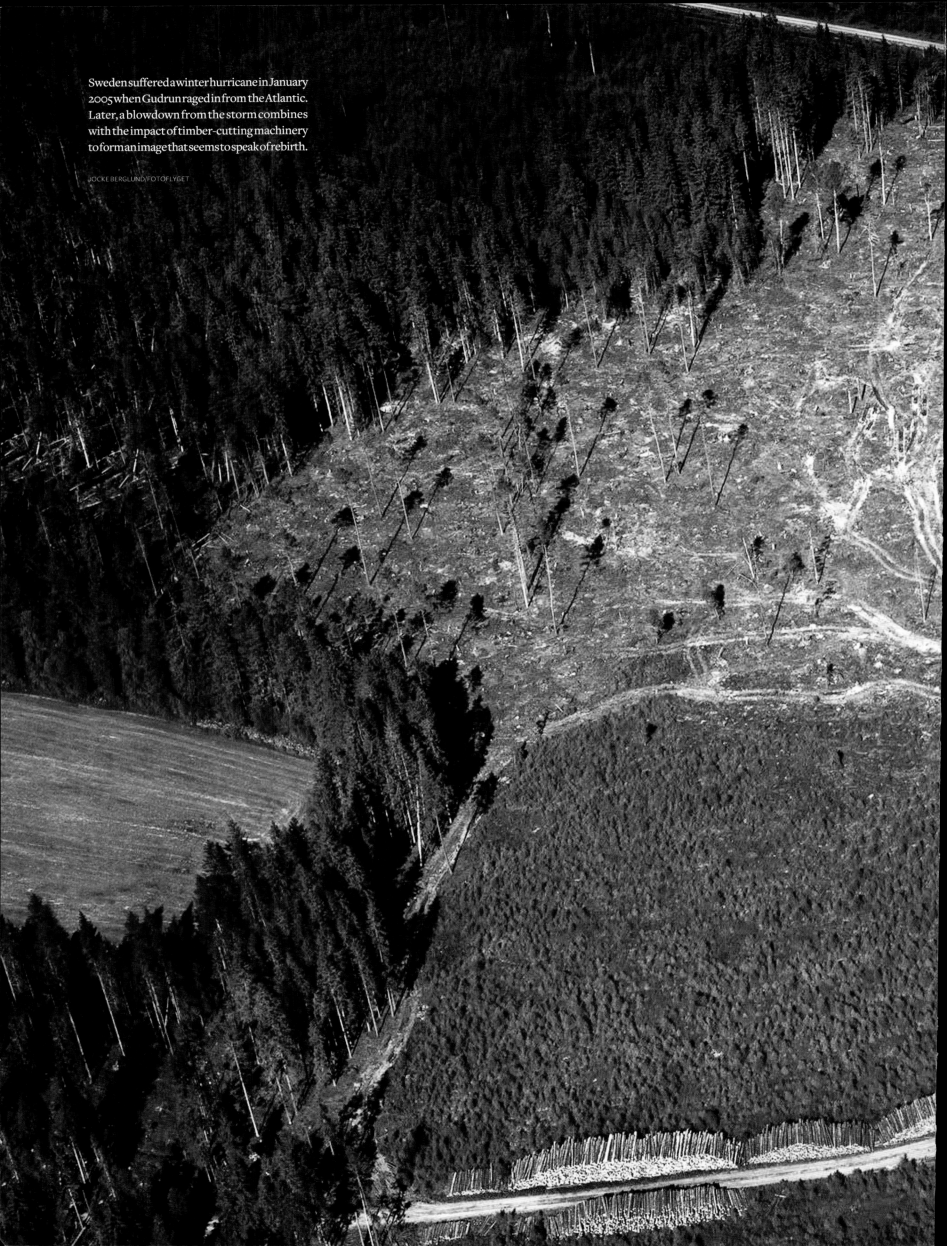

Sweden suffered a winter hurricane in January 2005 when Gudrun raged in from the Atlantic. Later, a blowdown from the storm combines with the impact of timber-cutting machinery to form an image that seems to speak of rebirth.

JOCKE BERGLUND/FOTOFLYGET

THE GREAT WHITE HURRICANE
1888

To qualify as a blizzard, a storm must sustain winds of 35 miles per hour for at least three hours straight, and falling or blowing snow must decrease visibility to a quarter mile. These violent conditions, hardly fit for man or beast, beset our country in lethal fashion not once but twice in 1888.

On January 12, the temperatures in the Great Plains, from South Dakota down to Texas, suddenly plummeted, the winds began to howl, and the snow started to fall. Hundreds of children were trapped in their one-room schoolhouses, giving the storm its name: the Schoolhouse Blizzard. Many of those who tried to make it home never did and were among the 235 who perished. Some people were buried under snowdrifts and not found until spring.

Bad as that storm was, it was not the worst of '88. The so-called Great White Hurricane hit the East Coast on March 12 and lasted three days. Fifty inches of snow fell in Massachusetts, and there were drifts as high as 50 *feet* in places from Maryland to Canada. Two hundred ships went down, and more than 100 seamen were among the 400 people who were ultimately killed in the storm. New York City, where another 200 of that total died, was the apex of the disaster. Fire damage in cities hit by the storm totaled $25 million because wagons and horses were unable to leave the firehouses. The Great White Hurricane is still, 120 years after the fact, considered the worst blizzard in United States history.

BROWN BROTHERS

In New York City, a young girl gives us some perspective when we see her against a mountain of snow (**right**); downtown, the spire of Trinity Church (**opposite**) seems to stand as a beacon while the storm rages around it.

THE JOHNSTOWN FLOOD
1889

This disaster was a collaboration between nature and man. On May 30, 1889, a rainstorm started in the western Pennsylvania county of Cambria, and during that day and night, it became a torrent, dumping as many as 10 inches in 24 hours. Years earlier, a dam had been built and a reservoir created about 14 miles upstream from—and elevated 450 feet above—Johnstown. In the middle of the afternoon on May 31, the 72-foot-high dam gave way, and some 20 million tons of water poured forth and headed toward the city.

No one knew what was coming. But soon they began to hear it: first a distant rumble, then a thunderous roar, as the wall of water, which had built to a height of 60 feet and a speed of 40 miles per hour, crashed upon Johnstown at 4:07 p.m. Lumber from shattered houses, boulders, dead animals—even people—were already part of the onrushing water, which would claim many more victims. Above the black wave, there was a swirl of spray that looked like smoke and would be forever remembered in the city as the "death mist." The historian David McCullough in his book *The Johnstown Flood* wrote: "The drowning and devastation of the city took just about 10 minutes.

"For most people they were the most desperate minutes of their lives, snatching at children and struggling through the water, trying to reach the high ground, running upstairs as houses began to quake and split apart, clinging to rafters, window ledges, anything, while the whole world around them seemed to spin faster and faster."

In all, 2,209 people perished in the Johnstown Flood. The minister of the local Presbyterian church, David Beale, wrote that the emotions of those who survived the tremendous deluge were simply inexpressible: "It were vain to undertake to tell the world how or what we felt, when shoeless, hatless, and many of us almost naked, some bruised and broken, we stood there and looked upon that scene of death and desolation."

JOHNSTOWN AREA HERITAGE ASSOCIATION

An uprooted tree is thrust into the Schultz family's house in Johnstown. Ninety-nine families were wiped out entirely in the disaster, and 98 children lost both parents. More than 300 men and women were widowed by the flood.

THE GALVESTON HURRICANE
1900

Dr. Isaac M. Cline was the meteorologist in charge of the United States Weather Bureau's local operation when, on July 15, 1891, he wrote in a *Galveston Daily News* article: "It would be impossible for any cyclone to create a storm wave which could materially injure the city." He noted at one point that, typically, hurricanes missed Texas, and those that did happen to come ashore were seldom very strong.

Cline's impossibility became a terrible reality nine years later when, on September 8, 1900, a Category 4 hurricane barreled off the Gulf of Mexico directly into the port city, carrying with it winds of more than 130 miles per hour and a storm surge of up to 20 feet. Over the course of 18 hours, the tempest mercilessly battered Galveston, which had a population of 35,000, finally leaving as many as 12,000 dead and 8,000 homeless. There were so many corpses, the overtaxed relief corps built funeral pyres throughout the city. More than a century later, the Galveston Hurricane remains the deadliest natural disaster in U.S. history.

Isaac Cline was still in charge of the Weather Bureau's Galveston outpost when the storm hit, and the good news is that he was, despite his earlier theories, clear-eyed about what he was witnessing. He raised hurricane warning flags on September 7, the day before the storm struck, and then: "Early on the morning of [the 8th], I harnessed my horse to a two wheeled cart ... and drove along the beach from one end of town to the other. I warned people that great danger threatened them, and advised some 6,000 people who were summering along the beach to go home

Against the backdrop of the ruined city, a schoolhouse sits (**opposite**), having been carried by the seawater for 200 yards before being deposited, miraculously intact. **Below:** Cline, who once thought such a storm couldn't happen, reacted courageously when it did.

ROSENBERG LIBRARY

immediately." During the storm, Cline and his wife, Cora May, attempted to shelter some 50 friends and neighbors, but their house was destroyed—and Cora May was killed. At that point, Cline "decided that I could be of greater service to humanity by determining what are the physical forces in the cyclones that develop the storm tides and by devising rules for use in forecasting and warning the public in advance of their arrival." This he did for the rest of his days. He died at age 93 in 1955.

MOUNT PELÉE ERUPTS
1902

The blast happened way back in 1902, yet 98 years later it still stood as the worst volcanic calamity of the 20th century.

It occurred in a theretofore sublime setting. The 40-mile-long island of Martinique is a mountainous, verdant Bali Hai in the Caribbean Sea. At the northern end of the island, stunning Mount Pelée, the highest of the peaks, rises 4,582 feet above sea level. In 1902, Saint-Pierre, Martinique's capital and largest city with 30,000 citizens, lay four miles south of the mountain and was influenced daily by Pelée's great beauty and large shadow.

Natives called Pelée "Fire Mountain," indicating that the cultural memory held that this was a volcano. It had been dormant for decades when, in late April, it began emitting ash and sulfuric gases. During the first week of May, the ebullitions became louder and could be felt more strongly in the city below; hundreds of venomous snakes, roused by the volcanic activity, took to the streets of Saint-Pierre, biting people and animals randomly. Soldiers were ordered to shoot the snakes, but no one could solve the problem of Pelée, whose eruptions built to an Ascension Day climax on May 8.

Shortly before eight a.m., the summit of the mountain blew, and two black pyroclastic clouds shot out at more than 400 miles per hour, one horizontally and the other skyward. The horizontal cloud raced down the mountain at astonishing speed and engulfed the city within a minute. Everything that the 1000ºF cloud of ash and gas touched turned immediately to flame. More than a dozen ships in the harbor burned and sank. Saint-Pierre, which would burn for several days, was obliterated.

There were two survivors—a prisoner being held in an underground cell (who was subsequently pardoned; he had been through enough) and a man who lived on the city's outskirts. Some accounts mention a third who lived: Havivra Da Ifrile, a young girl. Everyone else was dead.

Today, Mount Pelée remains the most active volcano in the West Indies, and it is fully expected to erupt sometime in the future.

Saint-Pierre, a cosmopolitan city of luxury and style, quickly became a charred ruin that recalled the remnants of ancient Greece and Rome. When put in historical context today, it reminds us of Hiroshima after an atomic bomb was dropped on the city.

What Is an Earthquake?

In 1760, John Michell, a British engineer and seismology pioneer, wrote that earthquakes and their resultant energy were produced by "shifting masses of rock miles below the surface." This long-ago conjecture was correct. The planet has seven major tectonic plates and about a dozen smaller ones; upon these sit all the continents and oceans. The plates represent a barrier between the earth's solid surface and its liquid core. Their various fault lines separate them from one another. Along these lines there is constant motion. This is slow but highly consequential activity: During the past 3 million years, movement along the San Andreas Fault on the California coast, which demarcates the border between the North American Plate and the Pacific Plate, has shifted at a rate of approximately two inches a year (about the same pace as it takes for a fingernail to grow). When the fault ruptures—when plates crash or pull apart, when the earth's crust is broken—energy moves in waves throughout the planet, and we feel the outcome on the surface. Earthquakes are measured by the Richter scale, which was developed in 1935 by Charles Richter of the California Institute of Technology. It registers earthquakes from micro (2.0 or lower) to massive (8.0 or higher). The largest ever recorded was the Chilean earthquake of 1960, a 9.5 that caused a phenomenon known as the free oscillation of the earth. Seismic waves traveled around the planet for days after the initial shock.

Opposite: Japan's Great Hanshin Earthquake of January 17, 1995, turns a highway in Kobe into an accordion. **Right:** A quake in Taiwan on September 21, 1999, claimed more than 2,400 lives and collapsed hundreds of buildings in the city of Chi-Chi.

SIPA

THE SAN FRANCISCO EARTHQUAKE
1906

n 1906, San Francisco, with a population of more than 400,000, was the largest city on America's West Coast. What happened to it shortly after five a.m. on Wednesday, April 18, was a disaster equal to what beset New Orleans when Hurricane Katrina rolled through it; both are pinnacle natural calamities in U.S. history.

The San Andreas Fault began rupturing at 5:12 a.m. under the waves of the Pacific Ocean, 90 miles northwest of the city, and the massive quake raced down the California coast at two miles per second. San Franciscans were literally shaken awake at 5:13; they leapt from their swaying beds to peer upon a surreal scene of buildings trembling and crumbling and debris raining from the sky. The earthquake rumbled on to the south—it would eventually carve a path of destruction 400 miles long—and San Francisco's nightmare had begun.

GETTY

Damaged electrical wires and overturned coal stoves sparked fires in a city where 90 percent of the houses were made of wood. Dozens of smaller fires merged into one, and the city's 585 firefighters were helpless in the face of the conflagration, not least since underground water mains had been destroyed. In a desperate move, it was decided that houses standing in the path of the advancing blaze would be destroyed by cannon fire and explosives, creating a firebreak 175 feet wide. Large sections of the city were saved by this savvy act, although it took four full days to extinguish all the fires.

Tens of thousands of refugees fled the city by rail, and many more constructed makeshift shelters on sidewalks, in the hills, wherever they could. As has been New Orleans's experience in our time, San Francisco's recovery was quite difficult. Two years after the earthquake struck, a tent city of homeless people still existed in Golden Gate Park.

To defray any doubts that San Francisco was a city worth rebuilding, officials originally reported 375 deaths, a ludicrous figure. Reevaluations have established a low estimate of 700 and a real possibility that as many as 3,000 perished.

As their city smolders, women pose on Russian Hill (**opposite**). Two of San Francisco's hallmark Victorian frame houses (**above**) were shaken by the quake. There was no Richter scale in 1906, but subsequent analysis has assessed the episode at somewhere between a 7.7 and a 7.9. One way to imagine it: This earthquake exerted a force equivalent to all the explosives deployed in World War II.

In modern-day San Francisco, every effort has been made to create an earthquake-proof city, but the San Andreas Fault remains just below the surface. San Franciscans realize this. They know what happened once could happen again.

Armed officers patrol Market Street. By and large, the citizenry behaved admirably in the aftermath. There was hardly any rioting, and as the famous San Francisco writer Jack London reported of the city's first terrible day: "Remarkable as it may seem, Wednesday night, while the whole city crashed and roared into ruin, was a quiet night.... There was no shouting or yelling. There was no hysteria, no disorder."

Jack London described "tens of thousands of homeless ones. Some were wrapped in blankets. Others carried bundles of bedding and dear household treasures. Sometimes a whole family was harnessed to a carriage or delivery wagon that was weighted down with their possessions." Here, a man gets a shave (**above**) and a group of people poses in one of the refugee camps (**right**) established throughout the city. The bonhomie was genuine, as the pioneering psychologist and philosopher William James learned when he walked through the streets of San Francisco. "Not a single whine or plaintive word did I hear from the hundred losers whom I spoke to," James wrote. "Instead of that there was a temper of helpfulness beyond the counting."

THE TRI-STATE TORNADO
1925

Nature's most violent storms are an American phenomenon. While India, Bangladesh and Argentina experience extreme twisters as well, the majority of these air funnels, which are spun out of especially powerful thunderstorms, occur in the U.S.

About two-thirds of the 1,000 tornadoes that form here annually are classified as weak, with winds of under 110 miles per hour and a life span of less than 10 minutes. About a third fall in the middle classification of strong, sustaining winds of up to 205 miles per hour. The biggest twisters, the 2 percent that qualify as violent, last at times more than an hour and cause 70 percent of tornado-related casualties.

An average of 60 people are killed by tornadoes in the U.S. each year. On March 18, 1925, 747 died and 2,298 were injured by a vicious outbreak of tornadoes in seven states. The Tri-State Tornado itself, the behemoth of those storms, claimed 695 lives in Missouri, Illinois and Indiana—more than twice as many as the second deadliest ever.

First spotted at 1:01 p.m. in Missouri, the tornado raced northeast at 60 miles per hour and crossed the Mississippi River into Illinois. At 2:30, it roared into Gorham, then plowed through Murphysboro, De Soto, Hurst-Bush, West Frankfort, Zeigler, Eighteen, Crossville…leaving 592 dead. The twister crossed another river, the Wabash, and went on to kill at least 71 more in Indiana. It was headed toward Petersburg when it died out at approximately 4:30 p.m. It had traveled 219 miles in all, which is still a world record.

Tornadoes look like nothing less than Mother Nature's killing machines. This monster was the most terribly efficient.

There was very little left of the town of Griffin, Ind., after the tornado passed through. Twenty-five townspeople perished; here, two survivors search the town's rubble.

THE DUST BOWL
1930S

America had experienced drought before. In fact, years of scant rain in the Southwest late in the 13th century certainly contributed to the disappearance of the Anasazi tribe. But in the sweeping saga that is the history of our country, no other weather-induced hardship looms as large as the Dust Bowl.

We were complicit in its creation. Throughout the Great Plains, the farming tradition was to plow and plant, plow and plant, with little thought given to crop rotation or other techniques that might preserve fertile topsoil. The farmers suffered no penalty for this practice as long as the rain kept falling, but when it stopped in the early 1930s, the exposed, poor-quality soil dried out—and then it blew away in the wind. In 1932, 14 dust storms raged throughout the Plains States; in 1933, there were 38. Some were enormous. On May 11, 1934, a huge storm seized topsoil from farms throughout the nation's breadbasket and deposited much of it on Chicago; a bit of it reached cities as far as New York and Boston. April 14, 1935, was dubbed Black Sunday after 20 storms erupted on the Plains. In writing about that terrible day, an Associated Press reporter gave birth to the term *dust bowl:* "Three little words achingly familiar on the Western farmer's >

In 1934, a "black blizzard" (**above**) overwhelms the town of Lamar, Colo. Such conditions and the agricultural ruin they caused forced millions to relocate. Among the refugees is this family from Texas (**opposite**), newly arrived at a California migrant camp.

tongue rule life in the dust bowl of the continent—if it rains."

By the mid-1930s, 100 million acres of farmland were ruined, heaping more misery atop the Great Depression that was already plaguing the country. Throughout the Plains and the Southwest, destitute farmers and their families took to the road in the largest migration in U.S. history. They hoped against hope to find ... something ... *anything*. Starvation was common for the remainder of the 1930s. The rains finally did return, but by 1940, with 2.5 million people having fled the Great Plains, the Dust Bowl had reshaped the nation.

Here, an eerie scene is captured near Boise City, Okla. The biggest of the many dust storms of April 14, 1935, was probably the worst of the decade. It was born in Wyoming, tore through Colorado and barreled into Kansas with winds of 60 miles per hour. For 40 minutes in Dodge City, mid-afternoon closely resembled midnight. In Oklahoma, where the storm's speed increased to 80 miles per hour, a funeral procession in Boise City came grinding to a halt. The storm moved on to Texas, scattering cars and sending people fleeing to their cellars. This frightful dust storm raised and deposited twice the amount of dirt and debris it would take to fill the Panama Canal.

AP

DOROTHEA LANGE/LIBRARY OF CONGRESS/PHOTO RESEARCHERS

DOROTHEA LANGE/CORBIS

Clockwise from opposite page: A happy child at a transient workers' camp in Texas; a mother and her children at a refugee camp in Nipomo, Calif.; hitting the highway in Oklahoma. The Dust Bowl, as slow-moving and dramatic as it was, attracted the attention of everyone, including many artists, who were inspired by it. The photographers Dorothea Lange and Horace Bristol and, for LIFE, Carl Mydans and Gordon Parks; the folksinger Woody Guthrie; and the writer John Steinbeck all wrestled with—and became associated with—this epic story. Steinbeck wrote touchingly in his 1939 novel, *The Grapes of Wrath:* "They streamed over the mountains, hungry and restless—restless as ants, scurrying to find work to do—to lift, to push, to pull, to pick, to cut—anything, any burden to bear, for food. The kids are hungry. We got no place to live. Like ants scurrying for work, for food, and most of all for land."

What Is a Hurricane?

Simply put, it is a large, violent storm that originates in a tropical region and features extremely high winds—by definition, in excess of 74 miles per hour. It also brings drenching rains and has the ability to spin off tornadoes. Why is it almost always born in the tropics? Because ocean temperatures must measure above 80ºF for such a weather event to get going. When warm seawater evaporates, the moist air rises, which forces the air below it into a low-pressure system. Air tends to move from high to low pressure, and in doing so, it creates tension, which is manifested as wind. The sodden air starts to revolve around the low-pressure system, which will become the hurricane's eye, usually 10 to 20 miles in diameter and free of rain or even clouds. Because of the earth's rotation, the winds swirl counterclockwise in the Northern Hemisphere, clockwise in the Southern, and they can reach speeds of more than 150 miles per hour. A hurricane can pack 500 trillion horsepowers; if 1 percent of its yield could be captured, it would support U.S. electricity and fuel requirements for a year. In our neck of the woods, we call these storms hurricanes. Elsewhere they are known as typhoons, tropical cyclones and even willy-willies. By any name, they are furious to behold.

On September 23, 2005, during the historic hurricane season that had already spawned Katrina, Benny Salas bikes on the pier at Galveston, Texas, as Category 5 Hurricane Rita churns up the Gulf of Mexico.

THE NEW ENGLAND HURRICANE
1938

Several names exist for this disaster: the Eastern Seaboard Hurricane, the Long Island Express or simply the Great Hurricane of '38. But we have chosen its most common moniker—the New England Hurricane—since a significant amount of the subsequent damage was inflicted upon the region, which is rarely besieged by hurricanes. In fact, before September 1938, the last one that the northeastern states had suffered in earnest hit in 1869. So when the New England Hurricane arrived, it seemed ferociously intent on making up for all that lost time.

Brewing in the eastern Atlantic, then gaining steam just east of the Bahamas, it reached Category 5 status on September 20 and began to race due north—to the considerable surprise of the U.S. Weather Bureau, which had predicted that the storm would drift into the North Atlantic. Five hundred miles wide with an eye 50 miles in diameter, it slammed into Long Island, N.Y., early in the afternoon of September 21, then moved at stunning speed (thus the nickname "Long Island Express") up the Connecticut River Valley into Massachusetts. Along the coastline, the storm wreaked the most havoc. The wall of water sweeping ashore was as high as 30 feet. In New York, it carried a Westhampton movie theater and 20 patrons out to sea; all of them drowned. The waves deluged Westerly, R.I., killing 100 more. The Savin Rock amusement park in New Haven, Conn., was engulfed, then swept away. More than 2,500 boats were destroyed, as were hundreds of seaside cottages and 26,000 automobiles. In Providence, the waters rose so rapidly that several people became trapped in their cars and drowned. This fast and furious storm's rampage lasted only a few hours but delivered a mighty blow.

At least 600 people were killed in New England and more than 700 in all. Some 16,000 homes and other buildings were destroyed, leaving 63,000 people homeless. Farms were obliterated, and 750,000 livestock were lost. The total damage estimate ranged as high as $400 million, and New England hoped it would not see another hurricane like this one for a good, long time.

CORBIS

Two women goof around for the camera in South Boston (**opposite**), but the storm was no laughing matter. In downtown Providence (**above**), cars are deluged as water levels climb as high as 14 feet.

THE CHINA FLOODS
2297 B.C. to the present day

As the words above indicate, this is a phenomenon: China has suffered several of the world's deadliest floods. In fact, on many top-10 lists of the worst natural disasters, Chinese floods account for several entries.

The two Chinese waterways involved in the most catastrophic floods are the legendary Yangtze and the Huang He. The Yangtze has claimed up to half a million lives during numerous floods in the past century alone, but it's still no match for the Huang He. The worst natural disaster ever was the 1931 Huang He flood, when perhaps as many as 4 million people perished. In 1887, flooding along the river claimed between 900,000 and 2 million lives.

The lethal combination of factors at work on the Huang He includes a silt-choked river coursing through the flat North China Plain and an enormous populace in its surrounding valleys. The Huang He floods chronically if not constantly; it has overrun its banks nearly 1,600 times in the past 3,000 to 4,000 years. Today, ever-higher dikes and levees try to hold in the Huang He, and a massive new system, the Xiaolangdi Multipurpose Dam Project, hopes to overcome the clogging silt that has plagued previous dams.

On two occasions, the Huang He floods were man-made. In 1664, the Ming Army quashed a peasant rebellion in Kaifeng by inundating the city, killing 300,000. And in 1938, nearly a million people died when, during the Second Sino-Japanese War, Chiang Kai-shek ordered the opening of a dike to halt the oncoming Japanese Army. These particular disasters were the most horrible—and *un*natural.

The Yangtze, seen here flooding Shanghai, is not a killer on the scale of the Huang He, but it's deadly in its own right. In the past century, flooding along the Yangtze claimed 100,000 lives in 1911, 145,000 in 1931, 142,000 in 1935, 30,000 in 1954 and 3,000 more in 1998.

LONDON'S DEADLY FOG

1952

Great Britain's Ministry of Health, in reporting the incident, made sure to cite London's reputation for fog, but then conceded—in a very British way—that, yes, this had been different: "In a city traditionally notorious for its fogs, there was general agreement on its exceptional severity on this occasion." Indeed, the so-called Killer Fog was the deadliest ecological episode in recorded history. It was also a catalyst for the environmental movement.

On December 5, 1952, a mixture of natural and man-made factors contributed to an otherworldly gray cloud that settled upon London. A dense mass of stagnant air had situated itself over the city as the thermometer dropped to near freezing. As the fog rolled in, an inversion layer formed and pollutants became trapped in the thick air, which grew darker by the minute. The frigid temperatures spurred Londoners to burn more coal, worsening the predicament. Schoolkids were let out early; moviegoers were sent home as the smog blocked projections from reaching the screens; at the famed Sadler's Wells, the opera *La Traviata* was stopped after Act I when the theater grew thick with haze. By Sunday, December 7, visibility on the streets of London was down to one foot. Only Jack the Ripper would love such conditions.

At first, most Londoners saw the fog as little more than a nuisance, but soon, as hospitals noticed an increase in emergency patients, the health ramifications became clear. Death rates spiked; on December 6, some 500 people perished. How many of them died because of the sulfur-and-nitrogen-dioxide-laden fog was, at the time, anyone's guess, but certainly respiratory conditions had been exacerbated. A Ministry of Health report estimated that 4,075 more people died during the fog than might have naturally. But subsequent analysis, including a study published this decade in the journal *Environmental Health Perspectives,* places that figure as high as 12,000.

On December 9, the winds blew in at last, and the four-day Killer Fog fled just as suddenly as it had arrived. But its effects lingered. The famous fog had made the dangers of air pollution crystal clear to people around the world, and soon scientists, activists and eventually politicians began moving toward new rules for a cleaner planet.

Left: A mother and her infant take a stroll through the normally scenic Hyde Park. **Opposite:** Two bobbies walk a lonely patrol outside a sweet shop in Piccadilly Circus. The city's iconic Shaftesbury Monument Memorial Fountain is barely visible in the gloaming.

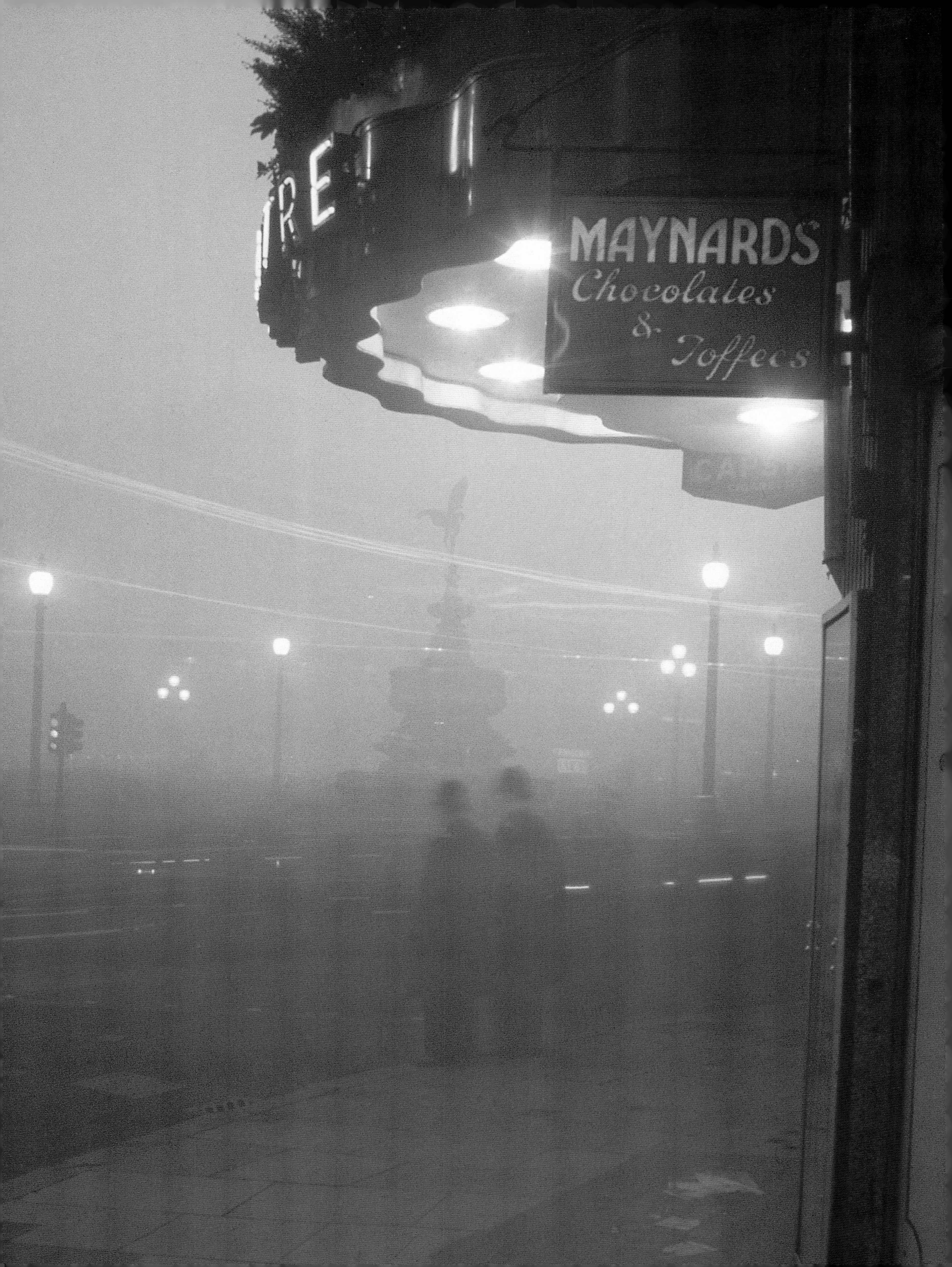
MAYNARDS
Chocolates
&
Toffees

THE NORTH SEA FLOOD
1953

From a satellite's point of view, the North Sea, a section of the Atlantic Ocean that's a bit more than 600 miles long and 350 miles wide, appears to be tightly lodged amid the surrounding landmasses. It is open to the north, then bordered on the west by Scotland and England, on the east by Norway and Denmark and on the south, where it funnels into the English Channel, by Germany, the Netherlands, Belgium and France. On the last night of January 1953, the sea was already experiencing a very high tide when a vicious northwesterly storm barreled over the top from just west of Ireland. It raced down the length of the North Sea, and as the body of water became narrower and shallower, an enormous hump of water formed in front of the howling winds. A titanic storm surge bore down hard on several countries, with England and the Netherlands in the crosshairs … *and hardly anyone knew it was coming.*

It was a Saturday night, and on such a night, most of the local weather stations were unmanned, and none of the radio stations were broadcasting. Many towns and villages were figuratively—and in some cases, literally—asleep. Then suddenly, they were underwater. More than half a dozen Dutch islands were overwhelmed by the >

Left: A Dutch woman and her son reflect the fears of their nation. **Above:** Along Nelson Road in Whitstable, England, police and civilians help evacuate homes. Even the U.S. Army came to the rescue, sending helicopters from a base in Germany to pluck refugees from rooftops.

sea; in all, more than 1,000 square miles of the Netherlands were inundated. The final death toll in that country was 1,835. In England, seawalls gave way, killing 307 people in Lincolnshire, Norfolk, Suffolk and Essex counties. Another 230 perished at sea on various vessels. The British ferry *MV Princess Victoria* went down in the Irish Sea east of Belfast, taking 133 lives with it.

As is often the case during disasters, there were acts of heroism. As other dikes throughout the Netherlands were being breached or giving way, the Schielandse Hoge Zeedijk was holding. Then, at 5:30 a.m. on Sunday morning, one section collapsed. Captain Arie Evegroen aimed his river ship *The Two Brothers* directly at the broken dike, and the plan worked: His boat effectively plugged the hole. Many lives were saved by this modern-day Hans Brinker.

In Foulness, England, a herd of cows finds an island sanctuary near a ruined farmhouse. Twenty-four thousand buildings in Great Britain were damaged or destroyed; in the Netherlands, the total was 47,300. Between the two countries, a total of 100,000 people were evacuated. Additionally, 30,000 Dutch animals drowned. Holland's government quickly and painfully discovered the country's vulnerability and launched projects to strengthen existing dikes and build new safeguards. These initiatives eventually led to the enormous Delta Works system, which manages the tides. Still, with North Sea waters rising in recent decades, future storm surges equivalent to that of 1953 are quite probable.

THE GOOD FRIDAY EARTHQUAKE
1964

Above: The fishing fleet in Kodiak is a jumble of destruction, wrecked by a tsunami. **Opposite:** Because the ground is still frozen, many of the dead, including this drowned longshoreman in Valdez, are buried at sea.

With a magnitude registering 9.2 on the Richter scale, this earthquake, which struck at 5:36 p.m. on March 27, 1964, was the largest recorded in North America and among the three most powerful ever measured in the world. The quake expended 80 times more energy than did the San Francisco earthquake, making the entire continent tremble; boats were damaged in Los Angeles and Louisiana. While only nine people were killed by the earthquake itself, subsequent tsunamis claimed victims not only in Alaska, where 106 drowned, but also at Beverly Beach State Park in Oregon, where four perished, and in Crescent City, Calif., where a dozen lives were lost.

LIFE correspondents traveled to Alaska and brought back vivid testimony. "All of a sudden the whole earth started shaking like crazy," said then-14-year-old Helen Irish of Valdez, "and the shaking got worse and worse.... The ground just opened up. Every time I took a step, I fell into a crevice. I looked down the street and saw the water. It picked up the *Chena* and tossed it like I used to toss boats in the bathtub. The two-story warehouse went flying up and crashed down in the water and disappeared. People on the dock were running, but the water just rose up and swamped them. Dozens of people just floated away…they just floated away."

FLORENCE DROWNS
1966

The human victims of this tragedy should never be forgotten: At least 30 Florentines died when the Arno River overran its banks on November 4, 1966, inundating the ancient and beautiful Italian city. Also, 5,000 families in the region were left homeless, and 6,000 shops were ruined. But, rightly or wrongly, this catastrophe is best remembered for the multitude of artistic masterpieces and rare books that were lost forever or badly damaged, and the worldwide effort of the so-called Mud Angels to save and restore the treasures that had not been swept away.

Heavy rains sent waters surging into Florence at 37 miles per hour, and narrow streets caused the flood to gain in height and intensity. The receding waters deposited 600,000 tons of mud and sewage, devastating the lovely city. At the Uffizi Gallery, at the National Library, at the Opera del Duomo … disaster. Cimabue's *Crucifix* was all but ruined, and Donatello's *Magdelen* was badly damaged, as were frescoes by Botticelli and Uccello. Some 14,000 works of art and as many as 4 million books were damaged or destroyed.

Florence cried out, and the world answered with money and volunteers. They could not restore everything. But with great effort, they restored Florence's pride.

The Madonna in the Basilica di Santa Croce (**opposite**) seems mournful. At one point, the basilica was surrounded by 22 feet of water. **Above:** Michelangelo's *David* stands above the flood in the Academia Gallery.

Scuba divers (**above**) return from a recovery mission in the Arno. Throughout the city—in the arcade of the Uffizi Gallery, in the cloister of Santa Croce—drying operations, like this one in a tobacco warehouse (**below**), were mounted. **Opposite:** A second *David* overlooks Piazza della Signoria.

What Is Lightning?

It is a spark—a long spark about as wide as a quarter—that can reach more than five miles in length, register a temperature of more than 50000°F (five times hotter than the surface of the sun), contain a billion volts (a bolt of lightning can keep a 100-watt bulb lit for months) and kill a person standing 10 miles away from the center of a thunderstorm (a "bolt from the blue") or someone who makes the mistake of picking up a phone in the midst of a strike. More people die each year in the United States from lightning than from the effects of tornadoes and hurricanes combined. At any given moment, somewhere in the world someone is being imperiled by lightning: More than a hundred lightning bolts strike our planet every second, and in a year, some 25 million lightning bolts emanating from 100,000 thunderstorms will reach ground in the U.S. How is lightning generated? Believe it or not, scientists still aren't sure. Generally speaking, it has to do with ice pellets forming high in a storm cloud that become polarized and—*whammo*—an invisible, negatively charged streamer races toward the ground to find a positively charged channel, such as a tree or a golfer, to complete its circuit. It is the bolt's brilliant return to the clouds that we actually see. Lightning, which includes any naturally produced static electricity, has also been known to occur during hurricanes, forest fires, nuclear blasts, blizzards and volcanic eruptions. Lightning is just waiting to happen.

From a blood-red sky above Tucson in the summer of 1992, lightning bolts are hurled toward the earth (and back) as if by Zeus himself.

KENT WOOD

THE BHOLA CYCLONE
1970

The storm is often called the "Bangladesh Cyclone," but when it struck, Bangladesh was part of eastern Pakistan. By the time George Harrison hosted a fund-raiser for the region in 1971, thus thrusting the disaster upon the world stage, Bangladesh had declared its independence, so Harrison dubbed his benefit the Concert for Bangladesh—hence the mix-up. The storm is, in fact, formally known as the Bhola Cyclone, after the Pakistani district that was most afflicted.

This tiger of a tempest roared ashore over the Bay of Bengal with winds of 115 miles per hour—equal to that of a Category 3 hurricane—on November 12, 1970. Its impact was catastrophic because much of the land it hit was situated near or below sea level. A dozen small offshore islands were simply wiped out. In the city of Tazumuddin, which is near the coast, almost half the population of 167,000 was killed. The relief efforts undertaken by the Pakistani government were in no way up to the enormity of the task, and in the days and weeks that followed, many more people died of disease, exposure or starvation. The final death toll of the Bhola Cyclone will never be known but is often estimated by reliable sources at half a million. The storm was and remains the deadliest on record—ever.

It was by no means the last time Bangladesh would suffer at the hands of a cyclone. In 1988, a storm flattened villages and killed thousands throughout >

In the aftermath of the storm, a man drags the limed body of a boy (**above**) to the river, where the current will carry it away. **Opposite:** A woman waits for rations that are being handed out by British troops.

the country. And in 1991, the properly named Bangladesh Cyclone, which was a lot more powerful than the Bhola Cyclone, packing winds as high as 155 miles per hour, sent a 20-foot storm surge over the land. At least 138,000 were killed, 1 million homes were destroyed, 10 million people were left homeless, and $1.5 billion in damage was done—but some lessons had been learned in 1970. Disaster shelters had been built, and aid was ready. In retrospect, it is clear that the consequences of the 1991 storm could have been much worse.

The storied LIFE photographer Larry Burrows, who was covering the Vietnam War at the time, raced to East Pakistan after the storm hit and took the pictures on these and the previous pages. (After finishing his photo-essay, Burrows returned to Vietnam and was later killed when the helicopter he was traveling in was shot down over Laos.) **Left:** Half-crazed from hunger, a mob surges into the stiff downdraft of a U.S. Army helicopter as it drops 10-pound sacks of rice and clothing. The pilot did not dare land his craft to distribute the provisions for fear the people would storm the copter and injure themselves. **Above:** Outside a shanty in the village of Sazerdee, medical aide Charu Chanson Saha inoculates a child (one of 500 to get shots that morning) against cholera, which was spreading through the delta.

ICELAND'S ENDLESS VOLCANO
1973

On a regular basis, volcanoes hold us rapt for days when a steady stream of smoke or a series of tremors indicates that something big is going to happen. But it is not often that a volcano stages an intense, long-term drama as fascinating as the one that occurred on Iceland's island of Heimaey in the first half of 1973. The episode unfolded at such a pace that we were able to watch a mountain forming right before our eyes. The pace also allowed intrepid islanders to leap into the breach to save the town of Vestmannaeyjar.

The eruption began on January 23 and continued for more than five months. It started with a fissure on the eastern end of the island, a rift that would eventually extend about two miles and from which lava shot at an initially alarming rate. Some 3,500 cubic feet of molten rock and tephra (the residue of airborne volcanic emissions) were spewed every second. A cone began to rise, and within two days, it was as high as a football field is long. (Today, this cinder cone volcano, called Eldfell, which means "Fire Mountain" in Icelandic, is more than 650 feet high.) The lava kept flowing, the hill expanding. The townspeople, living less than half a mile away, started to fret.

Most of the island's 5,300 residents were safely evacuated in the first several days, but as the eruption subsided, many locals decided to return and fight. A system was devised whereby seawater was pumped onto the creeping lava flow, which stopped it just shy of the town's harbor area.

Given lemons, the islanders made lemonade. They harnessed the energy of the cooling lava to heat water and provide electricity—thus, a disaster with a silver lining.

The sleepy island town of Vestmannaeyjar tries to get some shut-eye as Fire Mountain grunts, groans, growls—and grows—just beyond.

ROBERT S. PATTON/NATIONAL GEOGRAPHIC

Left: Not even 200 yards from downtown Vestmannaeyjar, the houses of many Heimaey islanders are entombed. **Above:** A car under siege. Some 70 houses and farms were buried under tephra, and 300 other buildings were destroyed by fire or lava. But at the end of the day, the saga of Iceland's endless volcano seemed, weirdly, a feel-good story. Only one man was killed, and daily life on the island improved—or so one could argue. Besides the natural power derived from the hot lava, the volcanic material, once it had thoroughly cooled, made Heimaey more substantial. The runways of the island's airport were extended, and a brand-new lava-based landfill eventually supported 200 houses.

ETHIOPIA'S DROUGHT
1973 to the present day

It seems as if every few years the images return to haunt our newspapers and evening newscasts: heartbreaking scenes of starvation from the latest African drought. Sudan, Somalia and other countries in the semiarid Sahel region have been afflicted, but none has been so woefully beset as Ethiopia.

What is at the root of these droughts, each of which has led to famine? Since it seems they occur on a kind of schedule, some scientists think that El Niño, the occasional temperature increase in the Pacific Ocean that triggers climatic variations worldwide, is the culprit. In 2003, the International Research Institute for Climate Prediction found "pervasive evidence" of a link between El Niño and these droughts. But in the previous year, another group of scientists claimed that air pollution from Western countries was driving the tropical rain belt in the Sahara farther south and blamed this for a 50 percent decline in rainfall in the Sahel.

Whatever the cause, the droughts are getting more frequent. In the 19th century, Ethiopia had a drought once every 10 to 15 years. Now it is every five years or less. The 1973 drought, during which as many as 300,000 died, grabbed the world's attention; the 1984–1985 drought, which killed a million Ethiopians, stunned us all. Since then, the country has experienced significant droughts in 1987, 1988, 1991–1992, 1993–1994, 1999, 2000, 2003 and 2006.

And there is no end in sight.

Famine refugees cross the desert in 1985. Pictures like this one and those on the following pages—from 1974 (**left**) and 1984— inspired relief efforts, including the famous Live Aid concerts.

SEBASTIAO SALGADO/CONTACT

What Is a Tornado?

This tremendous, funnel-shaped windstorm is a by-product of another storm, usually spun off by a thunderstorm or hurricane. Instability within the mother storm and wind shear (a change in wind direction and an increase in wind speed) in the lower atmosphere are crucial to the formation of a tornado, which often trails the storm that created it and is regularly followed by sunny skies. When cool air rides atop warm air, the warm air rises rapidly and the wind starts to spin; speeds of more than 250 miles per hour are achieved in the most powerful twisters. (The highest winds ever measured were during the Oklahoma City tornado of May 3, 1999, which produced gusts clocked at 301 miles per hour, with a margin of error of 20 miles per hour.) Since the conditions that create a tornado are very particular, these storms are common to specific regions. In the United States, for instance, although tornadoes have occurred in every state, they are prevalent in the so-called Tornado Alley running through the Midwest, Southeast and Southwest. Tornadoes are ranked by the Fujita scale, named for a University of Chicago researcher. It measures twisters from F0 to F5, from gale to incredible—which is sometimes also called violent.

On June 24, 2003, a massive F4 tornado rampages through the South Dakota countryside. This storm socked the village of Manchester, destroying every building but miraculously killing no one.

THE TORNADO SUPER OUTBREAK
1974

The phrase that best describes the 18-hour period from April 3 to April 4, 1974, in areas east of the Mississippi is "All hell broke loose." Meteorologists forecasted rain in the East and thunderstorms in the Midwest. However, 13 states—Illinois, Indiana, Michigan, Ohio, Kentucky, Tennessee, Alabama, Mississippi, Georgia, North Carolina, Virginia, West Virginia and New York—would be slammed with a torrent of tornadoes, a trail of twisters that stretched from the Canadian border to the American South and left up to 900 square miles of ravaged land in its wake. During the Super Outbreak, 148 confirmed tornadoes formed, a number never equaled before or since. The death toll was 330, and more than 5,000 people were injured in the chaos.

This perfect storm of weather conditions started on April 1 when a strong low-pressure system developed on the plains west of the Mississippi. As the system moved eastward, it collided with warm, moist air pushing north out of the Gulf of Mexico, thus creating an atmospheric mix that was growing ever more volatile by the hour. On the same day, several tornadoes of F2 and F3 intensity formed, foreshadowing the Super Outbreak. But no one could have predicted what was coming: supercell thunderstorms that would generate not just a remarkable number of tornadoes but extremely violent ones as well—six F5s, 24 F4s, 34 F3s. It was the highest quantity of violent twisters ever spun by a single weather event. >

At approximately 7:30 p.m. in Xenia, Ohio's Arrowhead subdivision, the big twister has already passed through as citizens run for cover after they're alerted to more twisters on the horizon.

WALT KLEINE/JOURNAL HERALD

On a day filled with astonishing occurrences, one ranked above all others. Outside Xenia, Ohio, several smaller tornadoes merged into an enormous twister that was half a mile wide and packed winds approaching 300 miles per hour. It tore Xenia apart, damaging or obliterating half of the town's 3,000 buildings. Thirty-four townspeople were killed and 1,150 were injured.

Well before 9/11, the term *ground zero* was often used in reference to disasters both man-made and natural. Xenia was the Super Outbreak's ground zero.

CORBIS

Right: The east side of Xenia is clearly decimated in the aftermath of the huge, superstrength twister. **Above:** Darlene Crane cries as she cradles her daughter Stacy. Crane, a resident of Xenia's Arrowhead subdivision, is reuniting with her three children after having been separated from them for 17 hours. The Crane home was destroyed by the tornado. Xenia was hit by another large twister—an F4—in September 2000. Fortunately, only one person died, while approximately 100 were injured.

BILL GARLOW/JOURNAL HERALD

THE TANGSHAN EARTHQUAKE
1976

Chinese scientists knew something was coming, but not only were they powerless to stop it, they weren't even able to issue a warning.

On July 12, in a hamlet outside Tangshan, an industrial city of a million people in the northeastern Chinese province of Hebei, a villager reported the smell of gas coming from a well. Later that month, gas was detected again on two successive days. Having monitored seismic activity in the area, forecasters at the Chinese Earthquake Bureau were convinced that an earthquake of a magnitude of at least 5.0—and probably much higher than that—would occur in or near the city between July 22 and August 5. Chinese authorities, wary of stirring any unrest in the country, what with the notorious Gang of Four in charge, ordered the information suppressed. On July 27, the well water in another village near Tangshan rose and fell, rose and fell. That night, residents of the city said they witnessed strange lights in the sky. Were the lights, perhaps, caused by the release of gas? Were they trying to tell the people what the scientists could not?

At about 3:42 the next morning, an earthquake rocked Tangshan for 15 terrifying seconds. Buildings throughout the city, hardly any of which had been built to withstand earthquakes, crumbled; 78 percent of its industrial structures and 90 percent of its residential buildings were destroyed or severely damaged by the initial quake and its several aftershocks. The first quake has been estimated at between 7.5 and 8.2 on the Richter scale by various sources. It was

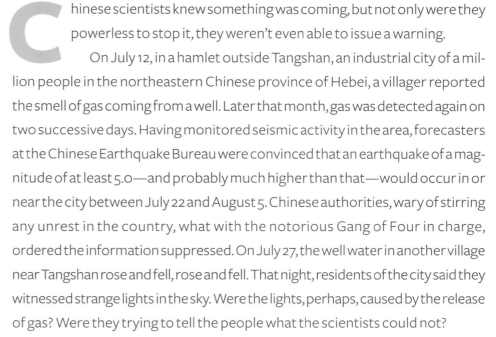

One of the 164,581 people who were severely injured by the quake is helped onto an airplane. Official casualty estimates for Chinese disasters are highly unreliable. Almost always, it is thought that the real numbers are larger.

followed 15 hours later by a deadly 7.1 shock and then a sequence of subsequent jolts that all registered greater than 5.0. According to Chinese officials, the catastrophe left about a quarter of a million people dead, but outside sources set the toll as high as 750,000. Either way, the earthquake in Tangshan was the deadliest of the modern era.

In October 1976, the Gang of Four was arrested, and China's brutal Cultural Revolution was finally brought to an end. If the earthquake had happened three months later, perhaps the forecasters would have been allowed to save tens of thousands of lives with a timely warning.

THE BLIZZARD OF '78
1978

As in 1888, when the U.S. got socked with two blizzards of historic proportions (the Schoolhouse Blizzard and the Great White Hurricane), in 1978 different parts of the country were buried by two record-breaking storms. On January 26, the Great Blizzard of 1978 blasted the upper Midwest, dumping as much as 40 inches of snow in parts of Wisconsin and forcing the Michigan State Police to pronounce Traverse City "unofficially closed."

A little more than a week later, a brutal nor'easter hit New England

BOSTON GLOBE/LANDOV; OPPOSITE: KEVIN COLE/BOSTON HERALD

and is remembered in the region today as simply the Blizzard of '78. This storm was remarkable for its intensity and duration: Stalled over New England because of a high-pressure system in Canada, it threw down snow for 33 continuous hours beginning on February 5 (a typical nor'easter lasts 12 hours at best—or at worst). Wind gusts as high as 65 miles per hour spurred tremendous storm surges in coastal areas: Both Cape Ann and Cape Cod on the Massachusetts coast were devastated, and many cottages were lost (2,500 houses were seriously damaged or destroyed in all). The enormity of the blizzard came as such a surprise that many folks were trapped out on the road. On Route 128, a circular highway outside Boston that is normally a steady stream of four-lane traffic, people died in their cars when rising snow blocked tailpipes. Fifty-four people were killed by the storm, many due to exposure. In Providence, bodies were found near the police station—victims who were within a few feet of shelter. A child in Massachusetts was caught in a snowbank just outside his front door and wasn't found until the melt.

Opposite: In Scituate, Mass., homes are left in utter ruin. **Above:** In Boston, alternate modes of transportation gain traction.

The dire circumstances of this uncommonly long storm, which dumped more than four feet of snow in some places and resulted in 15-foot-high drifts, brought out the best in many. Food deliveries to the elderly were made by younger folks with skis or sleds. The injured were transported to hospitals by Good Samaritans with snowmobiles. The startling storm even had a positive aftermath: Ever since then, when any big blizzard or hurricane begins to bear down on New England, the bread-and-milk runs commence. Supermarkets, knowing that the onslaught is coming, make sure to have an ample supply at the ready. Then the locals dash down the aisles and stock up. They remember '78.

What Is a Volcano?

G. BRAD LEWIS

This natural phenomenon is akin to an earthquake in that it often involves the shifting of the earth's tectonic plates. But it is different too. A volcano, of which there are several kinds, is an opening in the planet's crust whence molten rock (called magma below the surface and lava above), ash and gas are released. Many volcanoes, if you look at them simply as mountains, are made from their own residue: The lava cools and grows upon itself around and atop the vent. Volcanoes are prevalent along the boundaries of the earth's tectonic plates but are not exclusive to these regions. Wherever the planet's crust is thin, a volcano can form. There are volcanoes above and beneath the ocean surface. The island chain of Hawaii, for instance, is the product of volcanoes, and while active ones are today making the Big Island bigger, there remain underwater volcanoes that will one day emerge and join the chain as brand-new Hawaiian isles. Book your reservations now.

In these pictures taken on the island of Hawaii, the colors are vibrant and the lava is hot (more than 2000°F). In the mid-1980s, Puu Oo (**opposite**), the easternmost of Mount Kilauea's volcanic vents, erupts.

MOUNT ST. HELENS ERUPTS
1980

Harry Truman, an 83-year-old innkeeper, would not budge. He had lived near Washington State's Mount St. Helens for more than 50 years, and he wasn't leaving, even though the authorities were saying that activity beneath the grand 9,677-foot peak—a two-month series of tremors and ventings—indicated that the volcano, which had been dormant for more than a century, was about to blow. Truman's attitude was "Bring it on."

His body was never found.

Dixy Lee Ray, the governor of Washington, had heeded the scientists' advice and established a five-mile-wide red zone around Mount St. Helens. On Saturday, May 17, volcanologist David A. Johnston was working the overnight shift at the U.S. Geological Survey's observation post on Coldwater Ridge, five and a half miles from the mountain. On Sunday morning at 8:32, he was watching the ominous bulge on the snowcapped peak's north side. He saw it move. He excitedly reported to headquarters on his radio: "Vancouver! Vancouver! This is it!"

Those were his last words; he, too, was never found.

An effective red zone would have required a radius much wider than five miles. The energy expended by Mount St. Helens was 500 times greater than the Hiroshima blast. More than a cubic mile of lava, ash, pumice and rock was emitted; ash fell as far away as Oklahoma. A wonderland of nature was reduced to a gray wasteland. President Jimmy Carter, touring the volcano in the aftermath, commented, "Someone said it was like a moonscape, but it's much worse than anything I've seen in pictures of the moon's surface."

Mount St. Helens did not return to dormancy; in fact, it erupted 23 more times over a seven-year period. Here, on July 23, 1980, a plume shoots 60,000 feet skyward. On the next spread, an ash cloud surges on May 18.

As you can easily imagine, there is a story behind the photograph on the preceding pages, which first appeared exclusively in LIFE in July 1980: On the evening of May 17, Gary Rosenquist and four friends pitched a tent a few yards from the camper seen in the picture. At 8:32 the next morning, Rosenquist saw steam spurting from Mount St. Helens, fully eight miles away. Minutes later, the ash cloud began to surge straight toward his campsite. Before fleeing, Rosenquist and his companions banged on the windows of the camper to alert its sleeping occupants. Rosenquist then snapped the photograph through the windshield of his Datsun wagon as it was backing out. The couple in the camper also escaped, and they were lucky indeed, as the eruption treated all vehicles and houses like toys. A mobile home parked lakeside 11 miles from the volcano was tossed 200 yards. A crushed car (**right**) provides the only color amidst the bleak remains of a forest near the mountain.

THE MEXICO CITY EARTHQUAKE
1985

I t began at 7:19 a.m. on September 19,1985, 220 miles away on Mexico's Pacific Coast, and quickly fanned out in all directions. It was immensely powerful—8.1 on the Richter scale—and Mexico City, which had 18 million residents back then, was squarely in its path. From its epicenter, the earthquake took barely two minutes to reach Mexico's capital, which it proceeded to slam with powerful shocks every two seconds for about a minute. That is quite a long time for an earthquake to last, and in the never-ending minute, much damage was done.

As often happens in natural disasters (and life in general), the poor paid dearest. Most of the city's skyscrapers, several of which had been engineered to withstand earthquakes, swayed but did not buckle. Meanwhile, the tenements in the downtown slum of Tepito collapsed, as did Juarez Hospital, killing most of the 1,000 patients and staffers. A second hospital was badly damaged as well, while at a third, General Hospital, the obstetrics wing was destroyed and scores of mothers and babies died. The loss of these hospitals hampered efforts to care for the tens of thousands of injured.

The government put the casualty figure at 30,000 and said 9,000 had been killed by the quake, but few in Mexico City believed those numbers. Unofficial death toll estimates eventually ranged between 60,000 and 100,000.

At 7:38 p.m. on the following day, an aftershock jolted the jittery city anew. It was no usual follow-up but a sizable earthquake in its own right, measuring 7.5 on the Richter scale—easily big enough to cause additional damage and injury.

The government's response to the crisis was slow, but that of the citizenry was not. An army of self-proclaimed *Topos,* or "groundhogs," burrowed into the rubble and were still locating survivors in the remains of fallen buildings more than a week after the quake. In the wreckage of General Hospital, several "miracle" babies were found alive. Their rescue buoyed the spirits of the city when it needed it most.

The initial earthquake on the morning of September 19 claims this building (**right**) and more than 400 others. Thirty-six hours after the first quake, a family (**opposite**) is photographed at the very moment that a massive aftershock shakes the city a second time.

MOUNT PINATUBO ERUPTS
1991

For a long time, Mount Pinatubo had been a safe haven. Having last erupted circa 1500, it became, after the Spanish conquered the Philippines in the 16th century, the refuge of the Aeta tribe, who abandoned the lowlands for the mountain's deep forests. The Aeta called Pinatubo home for nearly half a millennium.

Then, in mid-1990, home became dangerous. On July 16, an earthquake struck Luzon, the Philippine island on which Pinatubo sits. The quake's epicenter was about 60 miles northeast of the volcano, and whether this was the spur that led to the eruptions will probably never be known.

In March 1991, there were earthquakes on the northwestern side of the mountain. In April, small eruptions from a mile-long fissure near the summit were followed by an increase in sulfur dioxide emissions, which lessened toward the end of May. Volcanologists were convinced that something was blocking the gas and that this blockage, and the pressure mounting below it, would lead to a big blast. Luckily, by mid-June, some 60,000 people had been evacuated.

There were explosions throughout the month, escalating to a series of four flare-ups between June 12 and June 14 that were extremely violent, and then one on the 15th that was cataclysmic. This eruption ranks as the second-largest volcanic event of the 20th century. Mount Pinatubo discharged 2.5 cubic miles of debris, including its peak and much that was within it. Some 800,000 tons of zinc, 600,000 tons of copper, nearly the same amount of chromium, 300,000 tons of nickel and 100,000 tons of lead, as well as other minerals, spewed from the volcano. >

The fallout was so thick it forced villagers to use umbrellas as shields. The ash cloud spread to the other side of the planet in two weeks and, within the next few years, affected climates throughout the world.

Locally, several hundred people were killed, but the volcano's reach would extend far beyond Luzon. First, the rains of Typhoon Yunya mixed with the ash to form a dense, muddy blanket that covered the area. Then those clouds began to drift across the globe, causing the largest stratospheric blip since the 1883 eruption of Krakatau created similar conditions. In the United States, the Mississippi flooded, and people wore sweaters on East Coast beaches in midsummer.

Two postscripts: The Aeta's culture was critically disrupted and remains fragmented today; Mount Pinatubo thereby achieved what the Spanish conquistadors could not. And as for the largest volcanic event of the 20th century? It was the 1912 eruption of the Novarupta volcano on the Alaska Peninsula, a place so remote and relatively unpopulated that the incident is all but forgotten.

In this photo and the one on the previous spread, the striking aspect is the sky. It was black as midnight above Luzon—but notice the shadows of the truck. This shot was taken in what should have been the light of day. The aerosols released into the stratosphere by Mount Pinatubo's eruption produced the worst ozone depletion ever recorded. Some scientists believe that the eruption led to yet another drought in the Sahel region of Africa. As the flare-up of Mount Pinatubo proves, once the residue of a natural disaster becomes airborne, nothing is "local."

DURIEU/SIPA

EUROPE'S HEAT WAVE
2003

We have seen violent weather hurl houses and vehicles through the air, cause inland floods and storm surges along coastal areas. A heat wave, by contrast, can appear benign and is often marked by high pressure and sunny days. But as the thermometer climbs into the danger zone and stays there for days—even weeks—on end, a heat wave becomes malevolent.

Since heat waves are hard to define, there is no list of the worst such incidents. But occasionally, a summer aberration is so extreme, it becomes a touchstone. Folks in the U.S. grimly recall two summers in the 1980s—1980 and 1988—when the heat was unbearable. A Chicago heat wave in 1995, which resulted in 600 heat-related deaths in five days, is also sadly etched in our collective memory.

The 2003 European heat wave might have been the worst in history. Whether it can be attributed to global warming will be debated in science journals for decades to come, but the effects are not in question. The most prominent of them: Between 35,000 and 50,000 people died.

In France, where summers are usually mild, temperatures on seven days in late July and early August exceeded 100ºF; because of this, 14,802 people perished. In Great Britain, 2,139 succumbed from August 4 to August 13. In Italy, nearly 3,000 died. Fires in Portugal claimed five percent of the countryside, 10 percent of the forests and 18 lives. Death was everywhere: Spain, Germany, even Switzerland, where a national record temperature of 106.7ºF was set and Alpine glaciers melted. The summer of 2003 was the warmest ever documented in Western and Central Europe.

In Brandenburg, Germany, on August 20, a field of sunflowers wilts. Approximately 7,000 Germans died due to the heat wave. Rivers in that country were reduced to their lowest levels in a century.

People beat the heat on August 5 under jets of water at "Paris Beach," down by the Seine River (**above**). A French woman in distress is counseled by Red Cross volunteers (**below**). The majority of heat-wave victims were elderly. **Right:** On August 10, an elephant at Munich's Zoo gets some relief. Untold numbers of farm animals and pets succumbed to the stress of the heat. Crops, too, suffered. In France, wheat shortfalls were 20 percent; in Italy, 13 percent; and in the United Kingdom, 12 percent. Interestingly, the heat sped up the maturation of grapes in European vineyards, concentrating the juice. The 2003 vintage, though small, is said to be exceptional—little consolation, certainly, to those who suffered through the merciless summer.

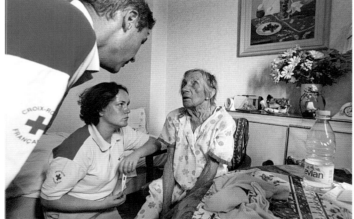

THE INDIAN OCEAN TSUNAMI
2004

Tsunamis—giant seismic waves that are often (and improperly) called tidal waves—can be caused by a number of things. They can be triggered when a large meteorite hits the ocean, but such occurrences are rare. Volcanic eruptions near or beneath the sea, like those on the islands of Thera, Tambora and Krakatau, can spur the humongous waves. But the majority of tsunamis are by-products of earthquakes, such as the killer waves linked to Alaska's Good Friday Earthquake in 1964. More than 40 years after that, on December 26, 2004, a 9.0-plus-magnitude quake 19 miles underneath the Pacific Ocean and about 100 miles from the west coast of the Indonesian island of Sumatra resulted in an unforgettable tsunami.

In fact, this catastrophe, also known as the Asian Tsunami or the Boxing Day Tsunami (because it happened the day after Christmas, which in current and former British territories is called Boxing Day), is formally referred to by scientists as the Great Sumatra-Andaman Earthquake. The tsunami killed people, yes—nearly a quarter of a million or more—but an earthquake so big that it caused the entire planet to shake was actually the culprit.

The waves traveled fast from the epicenter. A tsunami can move at 670 miles per hour in 30,000-foot-deep water; it can overwhelm nearby coastal areas in minutes and can cross the Pacific Ocean in less than a day. By the time the Asian Tsunami of 2004 was over, it would claim lives as far away as South Africa and Kenya.

It killed between 130,000 and 170,000 people throughout Indonesia, more than 35,000 in Sri Lanka, >

In the fishing villages and tourist resorts of Thailand's Andaman Islands, thousands were killed by a series of waves that kept crashing ashore for nearly a full hour. Here, in Koh Raya, the flight is on as a big one rolls in.

perhaps as many as 18,000 in India and 8,000 in Thailand. Somalia, Myanmar, Maldives, Malaysia and Tanzania all suffered lethal blows from the tsunami. Death toll estimates eventually placed the figure between 230,000 and 300,000, with 100,000 injured, some 50,000 missing and more than 1.5 million displaced. The second-deadliest tsunami in history, which was caused by the Lisbon earthquake of 1755, killed about 100,000.

There was nothing to do in the aftermath but weep and try to help. In the greatest outpouring of humanitarian aid ever, several nations pledged a total of $7 billion in support, and private individuals were just as generous. Thousands of volunteers sped to the region to do their part. The enormity of this tragedy was nearly equaled by the enormity of the response to it.

Left: A giant breaker storms the beach at Batu Ferringhi on Penang Island, Malaysia. The tsunami's waves, which appeared to be mere swells as they traveled across the open ocean, slowed as they reached land and then rose as high as 100 feet. **Above:** A man holds on for dear life on the inundated Thai island of Kho Phi Phi.

ARKO DATTA/LANDOV

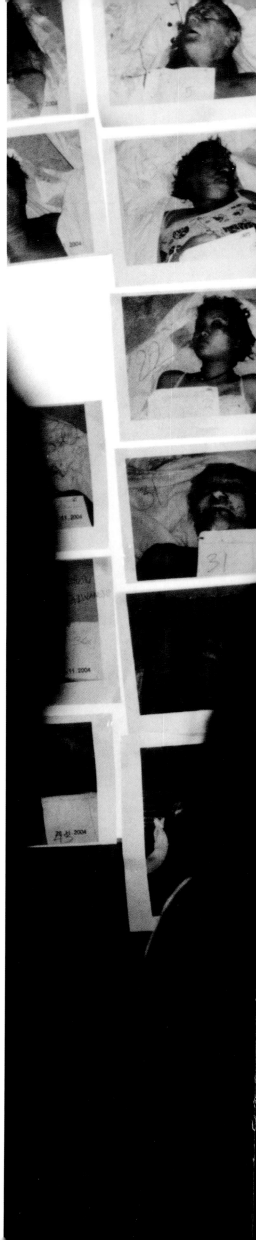

FREDERIC BELGEL/GAMMA/ZUMA

Top: An Indian woman in Cuddalore mourns the death of her relative. **Above:** In Thailand's Wat Yen Yao temple, volunteers and the Thai Army cover corpses in dry ice to preserve them from heat and decay, in hopes of eventually identifying the bodies. **Right:** At the Patong Hospital in Phuket, Thailand, relatives and friends desperately search for their loved ones among photographs of the dead.

PHILIP BLENKINSOP/VU

HURRICANE KATRINA
2005

A recent estimate claims that 1,836 people lost their lives because of Hurricane Katrina, so it wasn't the deadliest in American history: The Okeechobee Hurricane of 1928 took the lives of 2,500 Floridians, and the Galveston Hurricane of 1900 killed as many as 12,000 Texans. Katrina was only the sixth-strongest Atlantic hurricane and the third-strongest one to make landfall in the U.S. Yet it is widely considered our most devastating storm. The destruction and misery wrought by this tempest ruined a cherished and historic American city before our eyes.

Katrina was born in the Bahamas on August 23 in what was shaping up to be the vicious hurricane season of 2005. It became the second Category 5 hurricane of the year and, while at sea, intensified into one of the most powerful storms ever measured.

On August 29, Katrina, which had been downgraded to a Category 3 storm, made landfall in Louisiana and Mississippi. Despite destructive storm surges all along the Gulf Coast, the full brunt of the hurricane hit just east of New Orleans, so the city and the rest of the country initially thought a big bullet had been dodged. Then the levees began to fail. Nearly all of them in the metropolitan area were breached, and 80 percent of New Orleans and its nearby parishes and precincts went under.

The pictures on these pages tell the story of what we remember today as a slow-moving, excruciating, heart-breaking horror show, one of death, crime, terror, government ineptitude, constant, abject pain and occasional heroism. Having caused more that $80 billion in damage, Katrina was the costliest natural disaster in U.S. history. But the storm's final price cannot be measured in dollars. She struck a blow to America's heart and soul.

ERICH SCHLEGEL/DALLAS MORNING NEWS/CORBIS

The first priority after the flood was to get people out of the inundated area. Above are Katrina refugees arriving fretfully at the Astrodome in Houston, three days after the hurricane hit. They boarded this bus at New Orleans's heavily damaged Superdome, a huge indoor stadium that served for a time as an emergency shelter for shell-shocked residents. A year after the storm, a quarter of a million former Louisianans who had left New Orleans because of Katrina were still in Texas.

This page, clockwise from top left: On August 29, guests at the St. Louis Hotel in the French Quarter watch the hurricane rush in; a storm surge in a hotel stairwell; on August 30, Canal Street is a canal; on September 4, New Orleans resident Tom Cruise cries, "They're going to take my dog away at the airport," after being evacuated from his home via amphibious vehicle to a downtown staging area; a flag-draped body at City Park; also on September 4, Julie Duke cries alongside her husband, Randy, aboard a Black Hawk helicopter after being plucked from a rooftop; on September 3 at dawn, fires burn and a power outage keeps the city in the dark. **Opposite page:** Walking through oil-slicked floodwaters on the day after the storm. **Next spread:** On August 30, a neighborhood east of downtown is a picture of devastation.